Walking to Bethlehem

An Advent Journey

25 imaginative devotions
for adults and children

Fay Rowland

Visit the author's website at www.fayrowland.co.uk

Typeset at Attic Studios, England

Cover design © 2019 Elizabeth Thomas

ISBN: 9781702727495

Reviewers Say ...

"In the style of C. S. Lewis and Max Lucardo, this devotional and practical Advent Calendar will help you ponder the promise and ask the questions. Fun, festive and frank, this is a journey you are invited along."

"Travel from BC to AD with seeing, hearing and doing to focus your mind on the road to Bethlehem. Fun and devotional, practical and creative."

"In a light-hearted way, Fay brings the emotions and feelings of the characters in the bible stories to life. In the 'To Think About' sections, she helps us to imagine what was going on through modern eyes."

"Take a turn off from the Motorway Madness that is the rush to Christmas."

"You have made the trek before, but not in this way. Travel at your own pace, ponder, reflect and create, as you rediscover the walk to Bethlehem."

"This book will help you to think about familiar stories differently and put some well-known Christmas music into context"

Acknowledgements

Many thanks to all the folks who have beta-tested these devotions, who have suggested songs or illustration designs, and who have found ~~tpyos~~ typos. Particular thanks to David, Fiona, Lilian, Nicola, Richard, Sharon and Steve. You're a bunch of stars!

Grateful thanks also to all the good folks at Christ the King and St Botolph's with whom I have had the privilege of exploring God's world and word with families and children. God has greatly blessed me through you.

Thank you to the lovely community of scholars at Wesley House, Cambridge for insisting that even a mathematician can be a theologian, and for encouraging me to publish my work.

Special thanks to Steve for the constructive criticism, editing suggestions, endless cups of tea and occasional stolen Kit-Kat.

And most of all, thank you to my children, Emily, Elizabeth and Eleanor, who have put up with a mum always going tappity-tap-tap on a computer, and with meals of chicken nuggets and chips because I was too busy to cook anything else. (I don't think they minded.) They are the ones who inspired the original set of readings and are still the reason I do most of what I do.

Credits

Cover illustration by Elizabeth Thomas

Other images by the author or public domain.

Some of this material has appeared in larval form in The Reflectionary, a weekly blog of resources for interactive worship based on readings from the Revised Common Lectionary. You can follow The Reflectionary on Facebook (search for Reflectionary) or sign up to have the golden globs of goodness sent to your inbox weekly by visiting www.reflectionary.org.

If you like this book, visit www.fayrowland.co.uk to see other publications from the same author. You will find books of Bible sketches suitable for puppets or people, MP3 rehearsal recordings, academic publications and artwork.

Contents

What Is This For?

It's for making space.

Life is busy. Life with kids is busier still. Life with kids just before Christmas is … phew!

So take some time from frantic run-up to the festivities. Wind down and come on a slow journey to Bethlehem with Mary and Joseph. Savour the familiar texts and and put yourself in the story of the world's most famous birthday.

Starting on December 1st, each day has a short reading and a prayer, plus an imaginative reflection. There are also suggestions for music and relaxing colouring. You might like to build up the Stable Scene day by day, or move Mary and Joseph a step closer along a road or through a labyrinth. There are resources at the back to track the journey in creative ways.

Who Is This For?

Everyone!

Grown-ups and children, nativity ninjas and total newbies, tiny tots and wrinklies and everyone inbetween. There is something in these pages to help everyone engage with the story of Jesus' birth as if hearing it for the first time.

It is my prayer that all of us who use this book will discover new things about God and ourselves as we walk the road to Bethlehem, to meet the babe who changes everything.

Engage Brain!

Grown-ups sometimes feel that we have to leave our creative side behind when we leave childhood, but not so! God made our brains, and imagination can be a really useful tool for getting inside a Bible text.

The traditional Christmas readings can become bluntened by familiarity, so it is good to let the story really soak into your soul by reading slowly and thoughtfully. Using a different translation from your usual one can help as well.

Read the verses, perhaps a few times, and put yourself right in the action. What was it like then? What were they thinking? Where am I in the scene? What would I have done?

Come with me on the journey, whether this is your first time or your fiftieth.

How To Use This Book

Step 1 – Relax. This is not about 'doing' everything. There's quite enough 'doing' in the run up to Christmas already. This book is about 'being', remembering the reason for the season, not adding more stuff to your long list of stuff.

Step 2 – Read. The Bible passages are short and easy to read, so young children will be able to join in. Having short readings gives us time to savour every part of the familiar story, and helps us to take in some of the detail that we might otherwise skim over.

Step 3 – Choose. After The Bible Bit, all the rest is optional. Choose the sections that suit you. Perhaps you will think about the question in the car, or use the prayer during your lunch break or before bed. Perhaps you will have a labyrinth by your Christmas tree and move Mary and Joseph every day, or make the readings into paper chains or scrolls to hang in your tree.

What Is In Here?

The main part of this books comprises 25 devotions for the days of December up to and including Christmas Day. At the end of the book there are lots of useful resources and photocopyable pages for making your own family traditions for Advent.

Each devotion follows the same format, with many optional sections:

Stable Scene
A character to add to your Nativity display so that the scene builds up day by day. Follow the wise men on their long journey and see who arrives on Christmas Eve.

The Bible Bit
A verse or two from the Christmas story as told by Matthew and Luke, with linked texts from Isaiah and John. Readings are from the New Century Version, an easy-to-read translation suitable for all ages and traditions.

In The Action
Imaginative musings on the passage, putting us right in the scene. Some are a little quirky, some more reflective. Take a few minutes with a cup of tea and a biscuit, and let the wonder of the story soak in.

To Think About
A question to help us consider our own response to the text - challenging enough to engage older children and adults, yet accessible for younger children too. These are discussion starters rather than tests of knowledge. There are no 'right' answers.

Responding
A short prayer in simple language. Easy for children to read, but addressing real issues that face all of us. Suitable for personal or family prayers, or prayers from the front in schools or churches.

You could try writing your own prayers too. Putting words down on paper can be a great way to sort out your thoughts.

Listening
A varied selection of Christmas music that you might like to use to accompany your devotions. Some will be familiar, some less so.

Illustration
Colouring is not only for kids! Put on some music and grab your watercolours or pencils, then take a few minutes to think about the story for the day while you colour the illustration. I find it's a useful way to slow my busy mind.

You can photocopy the illustrations so that everyone can have a sheet. There are spare designs at the end of the book and blank versions if you want to make your own designs.

Counting Down to Christmas

This book started life as a way of marking Advent with my children. Normal Advent calendars are great for counting the days, but I wanted my family to have something a little more meaningful than chocolate snowmen and elf hats. I made mini books for my daughters, each containing one of the readings, and we hang one on our Christmas tree each day.

Here are four suggestions for using this book to help children (and adults) visualise the long wait for Christmas.

A Road

A great way to depict the journey to Bethlehem is with an actual journey to Bethlehem! Put numbers along the road (instructions at the back of the book) to keep track of the days, and move Mary and Joseph towards Bethlehem each day.

You can gradually build up a Stable Scene at the end of the rad as well, so that Mary and Joseph arrive there on Christmas Eve.

A Labyrinth

If you don't have room for a road, why not try a labyrinth? The journey through a labyrinth is the same as along a road, except that the it is folded up into a smaller area.

A labyrinth is not a maze. There is no puzzle, but a single, winding path that leads to the centre. There are no wrong turns and no confusion, only a pilgrimage.

Mary and Joseph can move through the labyrinth, pausing at the numbered stops each day. Even the young children can join in with this, following the numbers with the days.

There are instructions at the end of this book for making several different sizes of labyrinth that figures of Mary and Joesh can walk through.

Alternatively, you can print of one of the smaller designs and colour a section of the path each day to mark the days of Advent. You could even draw your own labyrinth based on one of the designs at the back of this book.

Scrolls and Paper Chains

Use the photocopyable resources at the end of the book to make 'antiqued' scrolls that you can hang on your Christmas tree each day as you read them. It's a fun craft as well as a lovely decoration.

You can also use the paper strips to make a chain that funtions as a count down calendar – a great visual reminder of the time left until the big day.

The Stable Scene

This is a wonderfully visual way to build up to Christmas. Each day you add a character or item to your crib, or move the wise men closer on their long journey. The wise men need four places to stay, the last of which should be close to the crib. This scene building works very well in conjunction with the road or labyrinth journey, but can be used separately too.

Characters

Here are the characters you will need:

Mary

Joseph

Jesus

Wise Men	(Balthazar, Melichior, Gaspar)
Angels	(Gabriel, Michael, Uriel, Zadkiel, Raphael)
Shepherds	(Laban, Amos)
Animals	(donkey, 2 sheep, 3 other animals of any appropriate type)
Things	(stable, manger, star)

Mary, Joseph, Jesus and Gabriel are named in the story. The wise men and other angels have traditional names, and Laban and Amos are Old Testament shepherds. Feel free to use the names or not as you prefer.

Building the Scene

Day 1	Add Gabriel (angel)		Day 13	Add donkey
Day 2	Place Balthazar (wise man) far off		Day 14	Add manger
Day 3	Place Melchior (wise man) far off		Day 15	Move wise men closer
Day 4	Place Gaspar (wise man) far off		Day 16	Add Michael (angel)
Day 5	Add stable		Day 17	Add Uriel (angel)
Day 6	Add sheep		Day 18	Add Zadkiel (angel)
Day 7	Add star		Day 19	Add Raphael (angel)
Day 8	Add sheep		Day 20	Add Laban (shepherd)
Day 9	Move wise men closer		Day 21	Add Amos (shepherd)
Day 10	Add animal		Day 22	Move wise men closer
Day 11	Add animal		Day 23	Add wise men
Day 12	Add animal		Day 24	Add Mary and Joseph
			Day 25	Add Jesus overnight

The Bible Bits

These are the Bible texts that are used for the 25 readings. You can turn the readings into paper chains or scrolls to hang on your tree if you like. See the Making Family Traditions section.

Day 1	Luke 1:26-27	God sent the angel Gabriel …
Day 2	Luke 1:28-29	"Greetings! The Lord has blessed you …
Day 3	Luke 1:30-31	The angel said to her, "Don't be afraid, Mary …
Day 4	Luke 1:32-33	"He will be great …
Day 5	Luke 1:34-35	"How will this happen …
Day 6	Luke 1:38	"I am the servant of the Lord …
Day 7	Luke 1:46-49	And Mary said: "My soul praises the Lord …
Day 8	Matthew 1:18	Mary was engaged to marry Joseph …
Day 9	Matthew 1:19	… he had in mind to divorce her secretly.
Day 10	Matthew 1:20	"Don't be afraid to take Mary as your wife …
Day 11	Matthew 1:21	"You will name him Jesus …
Day 12	Matthew 1:22-23	… Immanuel," which means "God is with us".
Day 13	Luke 2:1, 4-5	Augustus Caesar sent an order …
Day 14	Luke 2:6-7	The time came for Mary to have the baby …
Day 15	John 1:14	The Word became a human …
Day 16	Luke 2:8-9	Some shepherds were in the fields nearby …
Day 17	Luke 2:10-11	The angel said to them, "Do not be afraid …
Day 18	Luke 2:12	"This is how you will know him …
Day 19	Luke 2:13-14	"Give glory to God in heaven …
Day 20	Matthew 2:5-6	But you, Bethlehem, in the land of Judah …
Day 21	Luke 2:16-17, 19	So the shepherds went quickly …
Day 22	Matthew 2:1-2	Wise men from the east …
Day 23	Matthew 2:8-10	The star that they had seen in the east …
Day 24	Matthew 2:11	… gold, frankincense and myrrh.
Day 25	Isaiah 9:6	A child has been born to us …

Day 1 – An Eternal Plan

Stable Scene

Add Gabriel (angel)

The Bible Bit

Luke 1:26-27

God sent the angel Gabriel to Nazareth, a town in Galilee, to a virgin. She was engaged to marry a man named Joseph from the family of David. Her name was Mary.

In The Action

I wonder what excitement there was in heaven when the time came to put God's eternal rescue plan into action. I can imagine Gabriel stepping to the front of the crowd of angels.

"This is it guys." he says, "Today is the start of the biggest rescue in history."

"What do you mean?" ask the other angels, jostling to see.

"You remember God's plan to finally get rid of evil, destroy the power of death and rip down the curtain between him and humans? It starts today!"

The other angels are buzzing with enthusiasm. "Brilliant!" "I'll get my sword." "Can't wait to get into battle!"

"Stop, stop," says Gabriel, pulling back one particularly keen junior angel. "It's not going to be a battle. Well, not that kind of battle anyway. And it's only me going."

"You see, there's this teenager I have to visit. Her name is Mary."

To Think About

Why did God choose Mary, do you think?

Responding

Dear God,

thank you for your wonderful rescue plan.
You knew that we humans would go wrong and get lost,
and you planned to rescue us even before we knew we needed it.
Thank you for Jesus.

Amen

Listening

Rescuer (Rend Collective)
The Angel Gabriel from Heaven Came

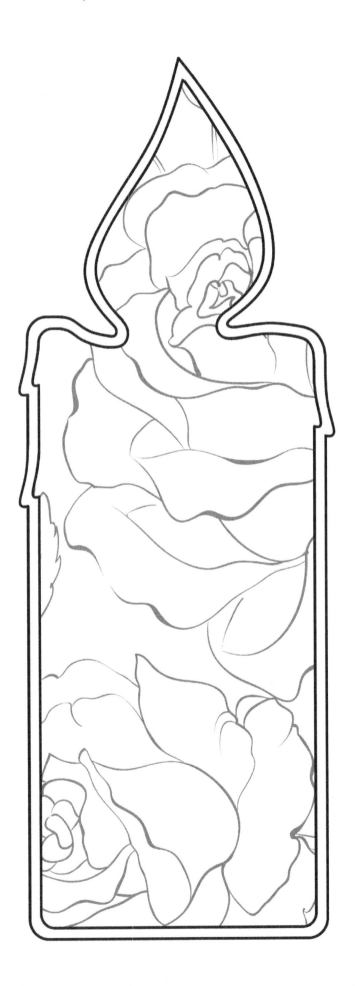

Day 2 – A Strange Greeting

Stable Scene

Place Balthazar (wise man) far off

The Bible Bit

Luke 1:28-29

The angel came to her and said, "Greetings! The Lord has blessed you and is with you."
But Mary was very startled by what the angel said and wondered what this greeting might mean.

In The Action

Imagine the scene: You are sitting at home, minding your own business, when there's a knock at the door. You put down your coffee / book / phone to see who it is.

And your jaw hits the floor.

There's a brass band outside your house. And a huge crowd of people clapping. And a film crew. There's a helicopter circling overhead, pom-pommed cheerleaders over to one side, and someone has let off a confetti canon.

And you're stood there in your slippers.

A guy with a microphone leaps forward. "Greetings, you who are highly favoured! The Lord is with you." he says, stuffing the mic in front of your face. Nothing comes out of your mouth.

"What kind of greeting is this?" you wonder, feeling an idiot as your gormless expression is beamed live across the internet.

I wonder how Mary felt.

To Think About

What would you have said to the angel?

Responding

Dear God,

thank you that you are a God who likes to talk.
Sometimes it's very easy to know what you are saying, like Mary hearing the angel.
Most of the time it's not so easy.
Help me to recognise your voice when you speak to me.

Amen.

Listening

Hail, Holy Queen (Sister Act)
Hail Mary Full of Grace (15th century carol)

Day 3 – Do Not Be Afraid

Stable Scene

Place Melchior (wise man) far off

The Bible Bit

Luke 1:30-31

The angel said to her, "Don't be afraid, Mary; God has shown you his grace. Listen! You will become pregnant and give birth to a son, and you will name him Jesus."

In The Action

What do you think about when someone mentions angels? Cute little blonde girls in white dresses and tinsel? Chubby babies with tiny wings and age-inappropriate archery sets?

Angels in the Bible are nothing like that. They are messengers, primarily, and usually appear as male. So think of a postman.

They're also soldiers, so give your postman some armour and a sword, or maybe put him in a tank or jet plane.

And most people are pretty scared when they meet an angel. That's why the first thing angels say is usually, "Do not be afraid." They're a bit gob-smacking!

So take your soldier-postman and add the most famous person you can think of (who you'd never dare talk to) plus a bit of that really hard test that you're dreading. Add smidgen of hungry lion, and I think you about have an angel.

Scary, eh?

To Think About

What do you think an angel might say to you?

Responding

Dear God,

Thank you that you know when I am afraid,
and that you promise to always be with me.
Help me to remember this,
even when I think I am alone.

Amen.

Listening

Mary's Boy Child / O my Lord (Boney M)
It Came Upon the Midnight Clear

Day 4 – The Promise

Stable Scene

Place Gaspar (wise man) far off

The Bible Bit

Luke 1:32-33

"He will be great and will be called the Son of the Most High. The Lord God will give him the throne of King David, his ancestor. He will rule over the people of Jacob forever, and his kingdom will never end."

In The Action

A lot of the time I have no idea what my children are talking about. I expect they feel the same about me. My eldest daughter is musical, and her talk of 'A-flat Demented' goes right over my head. However, we both like maths jokes. (Why is the horizontal axis called X? Because it is a cross!) In maths, we each understand what the other is saying.

I wonder how long it was before Mary understood what the angel was saying.

"You're going to have a baby," – Duh, I'm about to get married.
"He will be great," – I'm sure he'll be adorable.
"And will be called the Son of the Most High." – ummmn, son of Joseph, surely?
"The Lord God will give him the throne …" – hang on, throne? Why would a carpenter's son have a throne?
"… of his father David," – who's David?!? Oh, wait a minute, you don't mean …?
"and his kingdom will never end" – Oh, I see. *That* king. The one we've been waiting for.
The Promised One. Wow.

To Think About

What helps you to understand?

Responding

Dear God,

you always keep your promises, but sometimes we have to wait.
Help us to remember that you always do what you say,
even when we cannot see it yet.

Amen.

Listening

The Promise (Michael Card)
Come, Thou Long Expected Jesus

Day 5 – But ... How?

Stable Scene

Add stable

The Bible Bit

Luke 1:34-35

Mary said to the angel, "How will this happen since I am a virgin?" The angel said to Mary, "The Holy Spirit will come upon you, and the power of the Most High will cover you. For this reason the baby will be holy and will be called the Son of God."

In The Action

A bit earlier in this chapter there was another 'send an angel to announce a baby' thing. I wonder if that was God doing a trial-run. Perhaps he knew Gabriel would need the practice, because It didn't go so well the first time.

Zechariah and Elizabeth had been praying for a child for years, but when an angel popped by and told Zechariah that his wife would soon have a son, Zechariah didn't believe it. "Will this really happen?" he asked. "How do I know you are telling the truth?"

I can imagine Gabriel drawing himself up to his full (probably rather impressive) height, rustling his feathers and giving Zechariah a proper Hard Stare. "I am Gabriel", he says, "I stand in God's presence. And you don't believe me?"

Mary's question is very different. She knows that God will do what he says. She just wonders how.

To Think About

What question would you like to ask God?

Responding

Dear God,

I have questions. A lot of questions.
Some of them I have not formed in my head yet.
Thank you that it's OK to ask you questions
and it's OK to not know all the answers.

Amen.

Listening

Holy Child (Vineyard)
Infant Holy, Infant Lowly

Day 6 – According To Your Word

Stable Scene

Add sheep

The Bible Bit

Luke 1:38

**Mary said, "I am the servant of the Lord. Let this happen to me as you say!"
Then the angel went away.**

In The Action

Now here's a thought. What if Mary had said no?

"No, I can't be pregnant. My parents would be so angry."
"No, I can't do that to Joseph. He'd refuse to marry me, and I'd be disgraced for the rest of my life."
"No, it's too much to ask. I can't do it."

It would not have been unreasonable. Saying yes could have ruined Mary's life. It nearly did. 'No' would have been the sensible choice, the safe choice, the easy choice.

But Mary didn't say no. Mind you, she didn't say yippee either.

This was no easy task that God had put before her. It was not going to be a walk in the park. But she and her people had been waiting for this rescue for so long. How could she refuse?

Maybe God knew that she would say yes, and that's why he asked her.

To Think About

What do you think would have happened if Mary had said no?

Responding

Dear God,

thank you for Mary's courage and strength.
When you ask us to do things that are difficult
may we have the bravery and confidence to trust
that you know what you are doing.

Amen.

Listening

Mary, did you know?
Let it Be to Me According to Your Word

Day 7 – The Song of Mary

Stable Scene

Add star

The Bible Bit

Luke 1:46-49

**Then Mary said, "My soul praises the Lord; my heart rejoices in God my Saviour.
From now on, all people will say that I am blessed, because the Powerful One has done great things for me. His name is holy."**

In The Action

Mary goes to visit cousin Elizabeth who is heavily pregnant, and stays for three months to help with the birth. I wonder if Mary has heard the strange story of Elizabeth's husband, Zechariah, and his encounter with the angel. Perhaps that's why she went to visit.

I wonder also if Mary has told Elizabeth that she'd had an angel visitor too, and that she, Mary, was also expecting a baby. Or perhaps Mary is keeping that to herself for the moment.

But as soon as Mary walks through the door to secret is out. "Blessed are you among women, and blessed is the child you will bear!" Hugs all round and probably quite a few joyful tears.

Elizabeth's delight is catching. All of Mary's pent-up emotion comes flooding out and she bursts into one of the most famous songs in the Bible.

To Think About

What would your song be?

Responding

Dear God,

you have lifted up the humble
and filled the hungry with good things.
You have done great things for me,
and you show your mery for ever and ever.
Holy is your name!

Amen.

Listening

My Soul Proclaims the Greatness of the Lord (John-Michael Talbot)
Magnificat Anima Mea Dominum (Taizé)

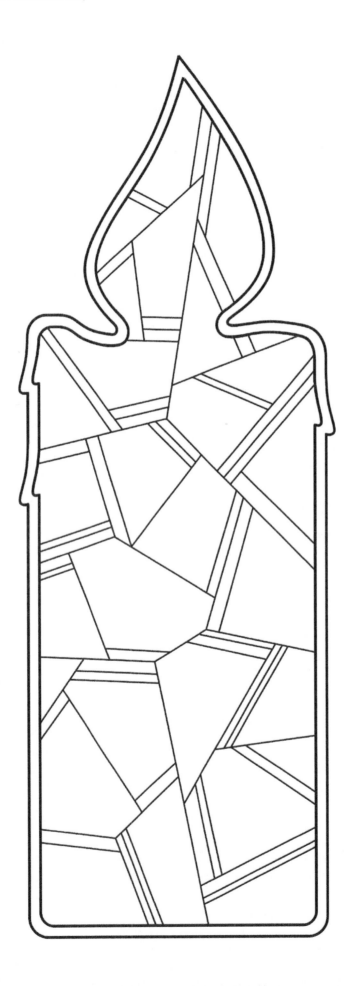

Day 8 – Back to Reality

Stable Scene

Add sheep

The Bible Bit

Matthew 1:18

Mary was engaged to marry Joseph, but before they married, she learned she was pregnant by the power of the Holy Spirit.

In The Action

Mary's song is a high point of the Christmas story, and I love the gloriously free expression of her joy. But now it all comes down to earth with a crash.

Joseph. He has to be told.

Did Mary tell him, or someone else? Perhaps the news got back from Elizabeth and Zechariah's. Or maybe Joseph spotted Mary's growing bump and worked it out for himself.

How ever it happened, there is now some serious talking to be done. How is Mary going to explain the baby? Does she tell Joseph about the angel? Will Joseph believe her?

I can imagine a knot of anxiety in the pit of Mary's stomach as she sits with Joseph. Her heart is breaking as well as his as she sees the disappointment on his face.

"How could she?" he is thinking. "I trusted her."
"Please God, tell him it's OK."

To Think About

What do you think Mary said to Joseph?

Responding

Dear God,

Sometimes we hurt the people we love.
It feels horrible and it's really hard to know how to make things better.
Please heal the wounds that we have caused
and the wounds in us.
Please help us.

Amen.

Listening

Somewhere In Your Silent Night (Casting Crowns)
Breath of Heaven (Amy Grant)

Day 9 – Disaster?

Stable Scene

Move wise men closer

The Bible Bit

Matthew 1:19

Because Mary's husband, Joseph, was a good man, he did not want to disgrace her in public, so he planned to divorce her secretly.

In The Action

What a dreadful decision. Joseph is a good man and wants to do right according to the Jewish law. But he also loves Mary and wants to do right by her.

If he marries Mary, people will think badly of him. No matter, he'll stand by her despite the nasty looks. But what would God think? That's the big question. Joseph can handle public humiliation, but to have God frowning on the marriage would be unbearable. No. He cannot not marry her.

But then what? Public disgrace for the girl he loves? She'd be thrown out of her father's house, and you can sure that no-one else would marry her. What then? Life as a beggar? He can't let that happen.

With a heavy heart Joseph chooses the best of a bad set of options. If he quietly cancels the wedding, perhaps no-one will notice. And Mary? He'll keep an eye on her, and make sure that she and the babe are OK.

To Think About

What would you have done?

Responding

Dear God,

Sometimes it is easy to choose between what is good and what is bad.
But other times there is only a choice between bad and bad.
Please look after people who are in difficult situations
and help them too find a not-so-bad option.

Amen.

Listening

Baba Yetu / Our Father
Millennium Prayer (Cliff Richard)

Day 10 – Son of David

Stable Scene

Add animal

The Bible Bit

Matthew 1:20

An angel of the Lord came to Joseph in a dream. The angel said, "Joseph, descendant of David, don't be afraid to take Mary as your wife, because the baby in her is from the Holy Spirit."

In The Action

Have you noticed how many surnames are something-son? The angel from Joseph's dream called him Joseph Davidson. But that's not his name. Look earlier in this chapter and you'll see that he was Joseph Jacobson. Did the angel visit the wrong Joseph?

Or perhaps the angel was looking more at the future than the past.

Sure, Joseph's father was Jacob. He was probably a carpenter too, and his father before him and his father before him. And that would be the plan for Joseph's eldest son as well.

But Joseph was also descended from King David, Israel's shepherd king. And that was more the heritage and career path that God had in mind for his son.

(By the way, there is a different family list in Luke. Some people think that one list is Mary's family and the other is Joseph's. That could be right because the word translated 'son' also means descendant, adopted son, or son-in-law.)

To Think About

How much do you think that the past determines your future?

Responding

Dear God,

it is amazing that you adopt us into your family
and tell us to call you Our Father.
You are the perfect Father.
Thank you that you call us your children.

Amen.

Listening

Once in Royal David's City
Baby Boy (For King and Country)

Day 11 – What's in A Name?

Stable Scene

Add animal

The Bible Bit

Matthew 1:21

The angel said, "She will give birth to a son, and you will name him Jesus, because he will save his people from their sins."

In The Action

Some names have meanings, but you never know if a name will suit. Call a baby Rufus (which means 'red') and there's no guarantee that he'll end up with red hair. Abigail ('my father is joy') could have a right grump as a dad. Joseph ('he will add') could be rubbish at maths, Hannah ('grace') could be clumsy and Mark ('from Mars') …?

My name means fairy, but I don't have butterfly wings and I'm not good at transforming pumpkins into carriages, so that's no good. However my nickname, Tigger, fits me perfectly because I'm bouncy and enthusiastic.

So what about the name that the angel gave to Joseph's son? Did it fit?

Jesus is our version of 'Yeshua' and it is the same name as Joshua. Both mean 'The Lord saves'. So I guess he lives up to his name pretty well!

To Think About

What name do you think that God would give to you?

Responding

Dear God,

You know me inside and out.
You see my heart and my dreams.
You have written my name on the palm of your hand.
Thank you that you know me.

Amen.

Listening

Joseph Dearest
Joy has Dawned

Day 12 – God With Us

Stable Scene

Add animal

The Bible Bit

Matthew 1:22-23

All this happened to bring about what the Lord had said through the prophet: "The virgin will be pregnant. She will have a son, and they will name him Immanuel," which means "God is with us."

In The Action

Choosing a baby name can be a tricky thing.
"I've always liked Cathy."
"That's the cat's name."
"Oh yeah. What about Teresa?"
"Our surname's Green, think about it."
"Good point."

So imagine the scene in the heavenly coffee bar when the Trinity were discussing names.
"How about Immanuel?"
"I thought we'd decided on Jesus. Is Immanuel going to be a middle name?"
"More a nickname."
"What, along with Prince of Peace, Messiah and all that? How many names does a kid need?"
"Yeah, but this one's important. It means 'God is with us'."
(Sideways glances across the table.)
"What, actually *with*? Literally with? In those messy lives that humans have?"
"Yup. Totally with. Right there in the chaos and confusion."
"You sure about this? It won't be easy."
"Nothing this important ever is."
"Good point. Jesus Immanuel it is."

To Think About

What must it have been like for God to become a human and live in our world?

Responding

Dear God,

thank you that you lived with us in all the mess and muddle of our lives.
Thank you that you left the glory of heaven to be with us so that we can be with you.

Amen.

Listening

O Come, O Come, Emmanuel
Like a Candle Flame (God is With Us, Alleluia)

Day 13 – Bad Timing

Stable Scene

Add donkey

The Bible Bit

Luke 2:1, 4-5

Augustus Caesar sent an order that all people must list their names in a register. So Joseph left Nazareth and went to Bethlehem in Judea, known as the town of David. Joseph registered with Mary, to whom he was engaged and who was now pregnant.

In The Action

This could not have come at a worse time. I wonder what Mary's prayers were when Joseph told her this bit of news?

"Seriously God, what are you playing at? Why did this have to be now? You asked me to carry your child, and it's not been easy, but I said I'd do it. And now this? I'm as big as a whale, my feet are swelling up like balloons and I need to wee every five minutes, and I've somehow got to walk to Bethlehem! Could you possibly make this any harder, do you think?"

Does that sound a bit disrespectful? Check out Psalms. There's plenty of yelling at God there. Plenty of telling God that life is not fair. Plenty of "why does it have to be like this?"

It's OK to tell God when you are cross, even cross with God. He knows already, so we don't need to pretend everything's fine when it isn't. It's OK to be not OK.

To Think About

What do you think Joseph said to God?

Responding

Dear God,

Sometimes following you is easy.
Sometimes it is hard.
Help us to stick with you
though the rough times as well as the smooth,
the same as you stick with us.

Amen.

Listening

O Little Town of Bethlehem
Little Donkey

Day 14 – Is That It?

Stable Scene

Add manger

The Bible Bit

Luke 2:6-7

While they were in Bethlehem, the time came for Mary to have the baby, and she gave birth to her first son. Because there were no rooms left in the inn, she wrapped the baby with pieces of cloth and laid him in a feeding trough.

In The Action

"I don't know what I else expected. He's a lovely baby, but ..."

"But what?"

"Well, after all the fuss with the angels and him being the world's saviour and so on, I suppose I thought he'd look ... I dunno ... different, somehow."

"Different? You mean you didn't expect him to look like a wrinkly prune?"

"Hey, show some respect. That's God's son you're talking about."

"My son too. Kinda. Is it OK if he calls me dad?"

"I'm sure that's fine. But ..."

"But what?"

"But he's so small, so helpless. What if I drop him?"

"You won't drop him."

"What if he gets sick? What if he gets a cut from your saw, and it gets infected and he dies?"

"That won't happen. We'll be careful. Anyway, that's years away. He's only been born a few hours."

"But how can I protect him and make sure he never gets hurt?"

"I don't think you can, Mary."

To Think About

How can God be a helpless baby?

Responding

Dear God,

you are so great and powerful, yet you became a helpless baby.
You are so majestic and awesome, yet you became like one of us.
Thank you for coming to meet us.

Amen.

Listening

Away in a Manger
Silent Night

From Heaven You Came / The Servant King
For Unto Us a Child is Born (Messiah)

Day 15 – Hidden Glory

Stable Scene

Move wise men closer

The Bible Bit

John 1:14

The Word became a human and lived among us. We saw his glory – the glory that belongs to the only Son of the Father – and he was full of grace and truth.

In The Action

Imagine the period of quiet after the stress and hassle of Jesus' birth. The mess has been cleared up. Mary's had a cup of tea and some toast. Someone has found a clean blanket for the baby.

No shepherds, angels or wise men have yet turned up. It's just Mary, Joseph and this new baby.

Is the baby sleeping? Crying? Feeding?

I wonder what he looks like. A big, chubby baby or small and slender? Does he have any hair?

What is Joseph doing? Perhaps he's putting his handyman skills to good use, trying to make something useful. Perhaps Mary is shushing him so that she and the baby can sleep.

And what is Mary doing? I wonder what she thinks as she looks at this little bundle of humanity cradled in her arms. Of course, every new baby is beautiful, perfect, a miracle. But this one …

To Think About

Put yourself in the scene. What would you be doing?

Responding

Dear God,

You made your dwelling among us.
You came to live in our neighbourhood.
You made yourself like us
So that we could see your glory.
That is amazing.

Amen.

Listening

Joseph's Song (Michael Card)
Light of the world (Here I am to Worship)
Noel (Chris Tomlin)

Day 16 – Awesome or Awful?

Stable Scene

Add Michael (angel)

The Bible Bit

Luke 2:8-9

That night, some shepherds were in the fields nearby watching their sheep. Then an angel of the Lord stood before them. The glory of the Lord was shining around them, and they became very frightened.

In The Action

When we think about shepherds and angels today it's quite a nice image – boys wearing tea-towels and holding toy sheep, girls dressed in white with tinsel in their hair.

It wasn't quite like that, in reality.

These shepherds slept with their sheep in the fields. They'd been wearing the same clothes for weeks and had not washed since … umm ... I can't even remember when. Part of their job was to fight off prowling animals, and they often got into scraps with other shepherds over grass and water for their flocks.

These weren't little boys in dressing gowns. They were rough men. They had faced down wolves. They had fought off hungry bears. And the tough guys were terrified of an angel? We can be sure that this angel looked nothing like a cutesy blonde 6-year-old with tinsel in her plaits.

Awesome? Yes, and Awful!

To Think About

What do you think the angel looked like?

Responding

Dear God,

These men fell to the ground in fear
at the sight of one angel.
But you promise that we will see you face-to-face,
and know you as you know us.
Wow!

Amen.

Listening

While Shepherds Watched Their Flocks by Night
The First Nowell

Day 17 – Good News

Stable Scene

Add Uriel (angel)

The Bible Bit

Luke 2:10-11

The angel said to them, "Do not be afraid. I am bringing you good news that will be a great joy to all the people. Today your Saviour was born in the town of David. He is Christ, the Lord."

In The Action

Final score, 3-0. Good news or bad? Depends whether you're Rangers or Celtic.

Everyone likes good news, but good news for one person might be bad news for another. Rain – great for gardeners, not so great for holidaymakers. Hot dogs for tea – good news for the kids, not so good for the dog. Oh, wait …

But here the angels bring a message that is good news for *everyone* in the world. Everyone. This is not simply good news, this is Good News, with capital letters!

This is something bigger than getting rid of the Roman invaders. This is something better than getting your dream job or marrying the one you love. This is something more lasting than winning a bazillion pounds. This is the best news that ever has been, that ever will be, that ever could be.

This is real, proper, everlasting Good News.

I wonder what it could be.

To Think About

What is it like to hear Good News?

Responding

Dear God,

Thank you that your Good News
is for all people, in all places, at all times.
Help me to be part of telling your Good News
to everyone around me.

Amen.

Listening

Joy to The World
Come Love Carolling

Day 18 – Perfect in Weakness

Stable Scene

Add Zadkiel (angel)

The Bible Bit

Luke 2:12

The angel said, "This is how you will know him:
You will find a baby wrapped in pieces of cloth and lying in a feeding box."

In The Action

Joseph was a carpenter. I bet he'd made a lovely little cot for Jesus, back home. I bet Mary had a load of blankets ready, and a cute little hat that Grandma had knitted. I expect they'd asked neighbours to come round and help with the birth, and someone was bringing them a stew for afterwards.

All those great plans, and what did they end up with? A manger. An animal's feed box. And a borrowed one at that. Could the baby not have come a week or two later, when they'd got back home? When they were ready?

But perhaps that's part of the story.

The Bible is full of people who didn't feel ready – Moses, Isaiah, Jonah – but God called them anyway. Mary and Joseph didn't have all their baby stuff. But the baby came anyway.

God does not mind if we don't feel ready. The Bible tells us that God's power is made perfect in weakness. I wonder what that means for me.

To Think About

What are your plans? Do you think they are the same as God's?

Responding

Dear God,

It feels safe to prepare and to have things ready,
but sometimes our own plans get in the way of yours.
Help us to hold lightly onto our ideas
And to be ready to change what we think we are doing.

Amen.

Listening

Calypso Carol (See Him Lying on a Bed of Straw)
Gloria / Angels We Have Heard on High

Day 19 – Turned up to Eleven!

Stable Scene

Add Raphael (angel)

The Bible Bit

Luke 2:13-14

Then a very large group of angels from heaven joined the first angel, praising God and saying: "Give glory to God in heaven, and on earth let there be peace among the people who please God."

In The Action

Sometimes God talks in a still, small voice, a sense of lasting peace, feeling of wholeness and home. God spoke to Elijah in a gentle whisper.

Sometimes God shouts like a trumpet blast. Moses got plenty of that in the burning bush, the plagues, and the fire and thunder from the mountain. Perhaps Moses wasn't very good at hearing the small voice.

I wonder how many times I miss what God is saying to me because I'm not very good at hearing the small voice. I wonder how many times God has slapped his forehead at my denseness. I wonder how loud God has to shout to get over the din of my life. I think I need to spend more time in the quiet.

God spoke quietly to Mary. God spoke quietly to Joseph. But the shepherds got the volume turned up to eleven!

There was no way you could miss this message, and it was a message worth shouting about!

To Think About

How can we hear God's voice better?

Responding

Dear God,

Thank you that you speak to us in the quietness of a sunrise.
Thank you that you speak to us in the power of storm.
Thank you that you speak to us in the beauty of birdsong.
Help us to hear your voice today.

Amen.

Listening

Hark the Herald Angels Sing
Glory, Let There Be Peace

Day 20 – Shepherd King

Stable Scene

Add Laban (shepherd)

The Bible Bit

Matthew 2:5-6

The prophet wrote about this in the Scriptures: 'But you, Bethlehem, in the land of Judah, are not just an insignificant village in Judah. A ruler will come from you who will be like a shepherd for my people Israel.'

In The Action

Kings and queens – what comes to mind? Crowns and robes? Huge banquets for important people, tables creaking under mountains of fancy food, and a dozen knives and forks at every place?

I don't know about you, but I'd feel very out of place at a banquet like that. I don't like wine, I'd forget to curtsey in all the right places, and I'd probably try to use the fish knife to eat my soup.

No, I'd be much more comfortable downstairs with the servants. Perhaps a nice pie for dinner, with mash and gravy, and as much tea as I can get down my neck. That's more Ike it!

But then – gasp – the Queen pops her head round the door. "Do you mind if I join you?" she asks, and slides into the chair between Jenny, the second under-housemaid, and Sebastian, a trainee gardener.

A Queen who scoffs pie and mash? Unheard of! A King who is like a shepherd? Nonsense!

To Think About

How would you feel if God invited you to join him at his banquet?

Responding

Dear God,

It is amazing that you, the ruler of the universe
can be bothered with ordinary people like me.
Thank you that you invite me to join your banquet,
and thank you that you won't mind if I use the wrong fork.

Amen.

Listening

The Lord is My Shepherd (Howard Goodall)
Do You Hear What I hear?

Day 21 – Talking and Thinking

Stable Scene

Add Amos (shepherd)

The Bible Bit

Luke 2:16-17, 19

So the shepherds went quickly and found Mary and Joseph and the baby, who was lying in a feeding trough. When they had seen him, they told what the angels had said about this child. But Mary treasured these things and continued to think about them.

In The Action

Have you seen the film *The Princess Diaries*? It's about Mia, a teenager who discovers that she is the heir to the throne of a tiny country. She tells only her closest friend, and secretly goes to 'princess classes' with her grandmother, the queen.

I can understand. She needed some time to get her head around it. A big change. Life wais never going to be the same.

However Paolo, the flamboyant hairdresser who prepares Mia for her first ball, 'accidentally' informs the press, and Mia's quiet life becomes a media circus. For Paolo, it is exciting news and he can't wait to tell the world. For Mia, it's a bit more complicated.

It's the same with Mary and the shepherds. The shepherds told everyone, "This baby is our long-awaited saviour!" Mary sat quietly and wondered what it all meant.

I can understand. She needed some time to get her head around it. A big change. Life was never going to be the same.

To Think About

Would you have told everyone, or thought for a while? Or a bit of both?

Responding

Dear God,

Help us to be like the shepherds, who were so excited at your Good News that they told everyone. And help us to be like Mary, who thought deeply about what the Good News really meant for her.

Amen.

Listening

In the Bleak Midwinter
When a Child is Born

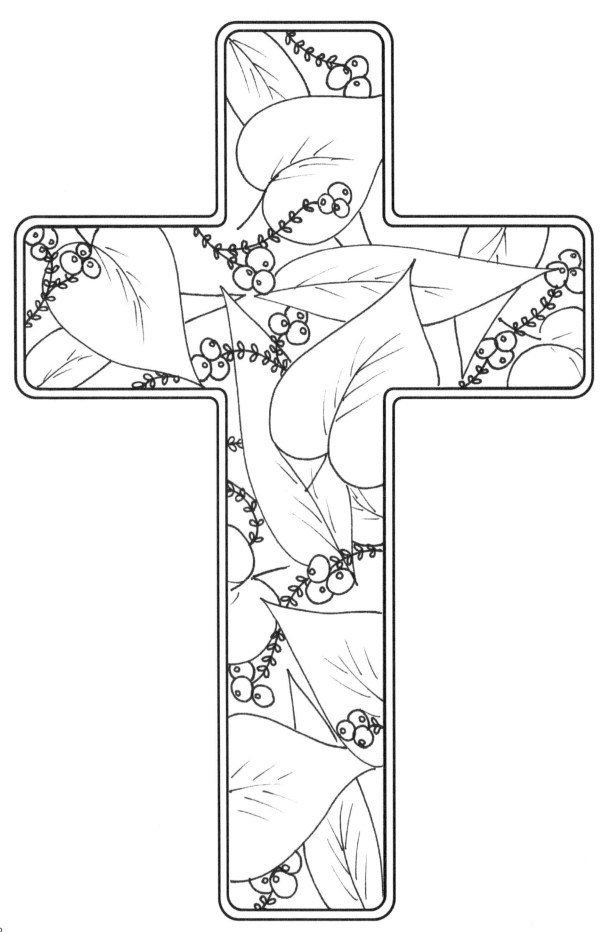

Day 22 – All May Come

Stable Scene

Move wise men closer

The Bible Bit

Matthew 2:1-2

When Jesus was born, some wise men from the east came to Jerusalem. They asked, "Where is the baby who was born to be the king of the Jews? We saw his star in the east and have come to worship him."

In The Action

I wonder what the wise men were thinking when they set out on their journey. They probably travelled from Persia, and that's a long journey to see a baby who is someone else's king.

Would they even be welcome when they got there? Persians and Jews didn't exactly have a happy history, so they might be turned away at the door. Perhaps the king of the Jews would refuse to see them. They were outsiders, after all. The whole journey might be a waste of time.

But time after time in the story of God's people we hear about strangers from other lands coming to worship God. Some of them are even listed in Jesus' family tree. And when Jesus grew up, he would shock the Jewish leaders by welcoming outsiders, by eating with outcasts, by forgiving the unforgiveable.

Three strangers come to worship. Perhaps they are not the 'right' kind of people. Perhaps they don't fit in. But all may come.

To Think About

Who might not fit in today?

Responding

Dear God,

thank you that you welcome all kinds of people into your family.
Thank you that you welcome me
with all my broken bits and weirdness.
Help me to spread your welcome to others
with all their broken bits and weirdness.

Amen.

Listening

As with Gladness Men of Old
What Star is This?

Day 23 – Star of Wonder

Stable Scene

Add wise men

The Bible Bit

Matthew 2:8-10

Herod sent the wise men to Bethlehem. The star that they had seen in the east went before them until it stopped above the place where the child was. When the wise men saw the star, they were filled with joy.

In The Action

The wise men were what we might call scientists today (although there was a lot of myth mixed in with their science). And although stars don't really tell us where people are born, or what they're like, God used the understanding of the day to guide these astronomers to the right place.

They were filled with joy at seeing the star, but were they filled with joy at where it led them?

I wonder what they thought when they found their journey ended here. A common house? Where's the king? Where are all the servants?

I wonder what they thought when they got their lovely robes dirty from the stable floor. Seriously? We came all the way here for this?

I wonder what they thought when they met the very obviously not-royal baby. It this it? Have we come to the wrong house?

Sometimes it's hard to see God when he looks like a human.

To Think About

Who can you see God in today?

Responding

Dear God,

you call us all to shine your light and to reflect your glory.
Help me to glow with your goodness so that others can see,
and help me to see your beauty in other people.

Amen.

Listening

O Holy Night
Stars (Skillet)

Day 24 – Weird Gifts

Stable Scene

Add Mary and Joseph

The Bible Bit

Matthew 2:11

They came to the house where the child was and saw him with his mother, Mary, and they bowed down and worshiped him. They opened their gifts and gave him treasures of gold, frankincense, and myrrh.

In The Action

What unexpected visitors! I wonder what Mary and Joseph thought when three wise men knocked on their door.

"Where will they park their camels? What can we offer them for food? I hope they booked a hotel because we certainly don't have room for them here!"

And what strange gifts!

"Errrm, OK. Thanks and all that, but what are we supposed to do with these?"

"Gold is nice, but we can't eat it. I could sell it, I suppose, but I'd probably get accused of stealing. I mean, why would a carpenter have a lump of gold? That's for a king, really."

"The incense is more use; we could use it to cover the smell of the nappies! But no, you're right. It's too special for that. This is the kind of incense that we burn to honour God."

"And myrrh? Oil for putting on for dead people? That's plain weird. Oh well, I guess they gave what they had."

To Think About

What do you have that you could give?

Responding

Dear God,
the wise men brought strange gifts to Jesus,
but that was OK with you.
I don't know if I have anything good enough to give,
but thank you that what I bring is OK with you.

Amen.

Listening

We Three Kings
Little Drummer Boy (For King and Country)

Day 25 – A Child Is Born

Stable Scene

Add Jesus overnight

The Bible Bit

Isaiah 9:6

A child has been born to us; God has given a son to us.
He will be responsible for leading the people.
His name will be Wonderful Counselor, Powerful God, Father Who Lives Forever, Prince of Peace.

In The Action

Overnight, something has changed. We did not see it happen. We did not hear it. But something changed.

Jesus is here. Jesus who came as a baby then grew to be a man. He has been here all through this journey, even when we could not see him. Immanuel, God-who-is-with-us.

So what do we do, now that the story has finished? It's Christmas Day, and all the characters have arrived in Bethlehem. I suppose everyone goes back now. The wise men return to their country. The Shepherds go back to their flock. Mary and Joseph eventually take Jesus home to Nazareth. But it's not back to how it was.

The wise men go home, but they have knelt before the King of Kings. The Shepherds go back to work, but they have met the Prince of Peace, they have heard angels sing of Good News for all people.

Reaching Bethlehem is not the end of the journey. It is the start of a whole new adventure. The story has not finished, it has only just begun!

To Think About

Where are you on your journey?

Responding

Dear God,

thank you for Jesus.
Thank you for sending him to live with us that first Christmas.
Thank you that he lived and died and lived again to allow us to be your children.
Thank you for Christmas.

Amen.

Listening

Saviour's Day (Cliff Richard)   Hallelujah Chorus (Messiah)
O Come All Ye Faithful   What Child is This? (Greensleeves)

Making Family Traditions

This book started life as a set of mini-booklets that I made for my children when they were very young. We still use them, and they've become a precious family tradition. The little booklets live in a fabric Advent calendar. We read one each day and hang it on our Christmas tree.

Here are four ideas for making your own family tradition, with instructions and photocopyable resources at the end of the chapter.

Advent Road

You can make a simple road and move Mary and Joseph a few steps along each day, arriving at Bethlehem on Christmas Eve. This follows the traditional 'Posada', an Advent custom in some Spanish-speaking countries, where large figures of Mary and Joseph move from house to house during Advent, arriving at church on Christmas Eve.

There are instructions below for how to make a road from sandpaper, and you can adjust the size to fit whatever space you have.

Advent Labyrinth

Iif you don't space for a road, you can coil the journey round into a labyrinth. A labyrinth is not a puzzle, like a maze. Instead it is a long path that winds around to the centre. Labyrinths have a long history in Christian prayer and mediatation, and are often used as mini-pilgrimages. You can stop and pray at each turn, or at other places along the path. A labyrinth helps us to think about how we are travelling, as well as the destination.

You can make a table-sized labyrinth with the Stable Scene in the middle and move Mary and Joseph one stop along the journey each day. Alternatively, you can print out a smaller labyrinth and colour in a section each day. Why not decorate it as well? There are photocopyable resources and instructions below.

Scrolls

You can make the daily readings into paper scrolls and hang them on your Christmas tree each day. You can make them look like icicles if you use silver and gold on the edges. There are instructions for how to make the scrolls, and photocopyable resources at the end of this chaper.

Paper Chains

A fun way to count down to Christmas is to make the readings into paper chains. You can either add one link to the chain each day until you have the full chain, or you can make the full chain in advance and take one link off each day. There are photocopyable pages at the end of this chapter to make your paper chains from.

Advent Road

You can follow Mary and Joseph's journey to Bethlehem by making an Advent Road. It makes a great visual marker of the long wait for Christmas, and children love moving the figures each day. If you build your Stable Scene at the end of the road you can watch Mary and Joseph get closer each day, arriving at Bethlehem on Christmas Eve.

You will need:

- Coarse sandpaper
- Stapler
- Green or brown paint
- PVA glue
- Moss or green yarn clippings
- Wooden or felt numbers 1 to 24

Choose how long and wide you want your road to be. It should be at least 20 times as long as it is wide. You could place it along a table or mantlepiece, or make it in sections to fit on window sills or even up the stairs! You could make it curved by joining sections at an angle.

Here are some approximate dimensions, in cm, if your sandpaper is 23 x 28cm (9 x 11"):

Number of sheets	Cut each sheet into	Each piece	Path length	Path width	Mary and Joseph move each day
1	5	5 x 28	130	5	5
2	4	6 x 28	200	6	8
3	3	8 x 28	240	8	10
4	3	8 x 28	320	8	13
5	2	12 x 28	270	12	11
6	2	12 x 28	320	12	13
7	2	12 x 28	370	12	15

What to do:

1. Cut the sandpaper sheets into long strips join them with staples.
2. Mix the green / brown paint with PVA glue and dab it thickly along the sides of the road.
3. Scatter moss or yarn clippings in the wet paint to give it texture.
4. Glue the numbers 1 to 24 evenly along the path, or mark small numbers with a pen for the locations of removeable numbers, so that you can take them away as you go along the road.
5. Place the road so that it ends at The Stable Scene. Mary and Joseph get to the end of the road on Christmas Eve.
6. If you like, you can place the other figures along the road on the appropriate days (see The Stable Scene for a list of chacters and days). You can add the figures to the Stable Scene as Mary and Joseph meet them on the road.

Advent Labyrinth

A labyrinth is like a road, but coiled up to take less room. You can use the photocopyable pages at the end of this chapter for a small, colour-in labyrinth. There are several designs to choose from, and you can add your own decorations.

Alternatively, make a table-sized labyrinth and use the Mary and Joseph characters from the Stable Scene to walk through it. If you have room, you can build the Stable Scene in the middle so that Mary and Jospeh arrive there on Christmas Eve.

You will Need:

- Fabric, felt, wood or carpet off-cut
- Pencil or washable marker
- Paints or marker pens
- Ruler
- String
- Wooden or felt numbers 1 to 24

Choose how wide you want your finished labyrinth to be, and how wide you want the centre and paths. Here are some suggested dimensions, in cm:

Outside diameter	Path width	Centre diameter	Circle radii							
40	2	12	6	8	10	12	14	16	18	20
60	3	18	9	12	15	18	21	24	27	30
80	4	24	12	16	20	24	28	32	36	40
100	5	30	15	20	25	30	35	40	45	50

What to Do:

1. Use the pencil and string to mark the largest circle on your material. Cut it out and neaten the edges if necessary.

2. Lightly mark the other circles, making sure they have the same centre. Do not make these lines too dark because you will only need parts of them.

3. Lightly mark lines from the centre to the edge at the quarters: top, bottom (the entrance), right and left.

4. You also will need one vertical line to the left of the line for the entrance, and one to the right. These make the paths for the way in and the way to the centre. Make the paths the same width as the gaps between your circles.

5. Following the pattern, erase parts of the cicles and lines, making all gaps the same width as the gap between your circles.

6. When you are sure you have the lines right, go over them in permanent marker, paint or yarn if you are using fabric or felt. You can add 'blobs' to the ends of lines if you want.

7. Add your date markers at the places shown on the pattern. You can paint the numbers on, or glue on felt or wooden numbers. Alternatively, mark small numbers on the labyrinth and have larger removeable numbers, perhaps on slices of wood, that you can take away as you walk along the path day by day.

Scrolls

You will need:

- 25 daily readings (see next pages)
- Tea bag
- Ribbon or string for hanging

What to do:

1. Print out the readings onto white or coloured paper. Do not trim the edges.
2. Dip a finger in some water and draw wet lines around the readings. Let the paper soak for a minute, then carefully tear the readings apart down the wet lines, giving ragged edges.
3. Soak a tea bag in water and use it to 'age' the paper. You can either dab the tea bag all over the paper (this looks best on white) or dab only the torn edges.
4. Roll the paper strips up, starting from the not-number end, and leave them to dry.
5. Add hanging loops to the corners near the number (punch a hole or attach with tape) and store your scrolls in a box, ready to hang on the tree each day.

Paper Chains

You will need:

- 25 daily readings (see next pages)
- Scissors (possibly wavy ones)
- Coloured pens
- Glue

What to do:

1. Print out the readings onto coloured paper and trim the edges.
2. Cut the readings into long strips, with stright or wavy edges.
3. Use pens to highlight the edges, or decorate the backs of the strips.
4. Glue each strip into a loop, threading each loop through yesterday's to make a chain.

You have two options with a paper chain: as a count-down calendar, or a count-up.

To count up to Christmas, have the strips in a pile and add one to the chain each day until you have the whole story chain on Christmas Day. For a count-down calendar, make the whole chain in advance and carefully cut one strip from the chain each day. When you have read it, you could roll it into a scroll to hang on the tree if you like.

Copyable Resources

The 25 readings are jumbled up so that they look good if you copy them onto different colours of paper. After the readings, there are some additional colouring pages and blank templates if you want to make your own designs. Finally, there are some labyrinth designs.

If you own this book, you may reproduce any pages marked as copyable for your own use in family, educational and religious contexts. Visit www.fayrowland.co.uk for high-resolution digital versions which you may use under the same conditions. You may not otherwise distribute pages, whether commercially or not.

1 God sent the angel Gabriel to Nazareth, a town in Galilee, to a virgin. She was engaged to marry a man named Joseph from the family of David. Her name was Mary.   Luke 1:26-27

6 "I Mary said, "I am the servant of the Lord. Let this happen to me as you say!" Then the angel went away. Luke 1:38

11 "S The angel said, "She will give birth to a son, and you will name him Jesus, because he will save his people from their sins." Matthew 1:21

16 An That night, some shepherds were in the fields nearby watching their sheep. Then an angel of the Lord stood before them. The glory of the Lord was shining around them, and they became very frightened.   Luke 2:8-9

21 So So the shepherds went quickly and found Mary and Joseph and the baby, who was lying in a feeding trough. When they had seen him, they told what the angels had said about this child. But Mary treasured these things and continued to think about them. Luke 2:16-17, 19

2 The angel came to her and said, "Greetings! The Lord has blessed you and is with you." But Mary was very startled by what the angel said and wondered what this greeting might mean.   Luke 1:28-29

7 Then Mary said, "My soul praises the Lord; my heart rejoices in God my Saviour. From now on, all people will say that I am blessed, because the Powerful One has done great things for me. His name is holy."   Luke 1:46-49

12 All this happened to bring about what the Lord had said through the prophet: "The virgin will be pregnant. She will have a son, and they will name him Immanuel," which means "God is with us."   Matthew 1:22-23

17 The angel said to them, "Do not be afraid. I am bringing you good news that will be a great joy to all the people. Today your Saviour was born in the town of David. He is Christ, the Lord."   Luke 2:10-11

22 When Jesus was born, some wise men from the east came to Jerusalem. They asked, "Where is the baby who was born to be the king of the Jews? We saw his star in the east and have come to worship him."   Matthew 2:1-2

3

The angel said to her, "Don't be afraid, Mary; God has shown you his grace. Listen! You will become pregnant and give birth to a son, and you will name him Jesus."   Luke 1:30-31

8

M Mary was engaged to marry Joseph, but before they married, she learned she was pregnant by the power of the Holy Spirit. Matthew 1:18

13

Augustus Caesar sent an order that all people must list their names in a register. So Joseph left Nazareth and went to Bethlehem in Judea, known as the town of David. Joseph registered with Mary, to whom he was engaged and who was now pregnant.   Luke 2:1-5

18

The angel said, "This is how you will know him: You will find a baby wrapped in pieces of cloth and lying in a feeding box." Luke 2:12

23

Herod sent the wise men to Bethlehem. The star that they had seen in the east went before them until it stopped above the place where the child was. When the wise men saw the star, they were filled with joy.   Matthew 2:8-10

4 "He will be great and will be called the Son of the Most High. The Lord God will give him the throne of King David, his ancestor. He will rule over the people of Jacob forever, and his kingdom will never end." Luke 1:32-33

9 Because Mary's husband, Joseph, was a good man, he did not want to disgrace her in public, so he planned to divorce her secretly. Matthew 1:19

14 While they were in Bethlehem, the time came for Mary to have the baby, and she gave birth to her first son. Because there were no rooms left in the inn, she wrapped the baby with pieces of cloth and laid him in a feeding trough. Luke 2:6-7

19 Then a very large group of angels from heaven joined the first angel, praising God and saying: "Give glory to God in heaven, and on earth let there be peace among the people who please God." Luke 2:13-14

24 They came to the house where the child was and saw him with his mother, Mary, and they bowed down and worshiped him. They opened their gifts and gave him treasures of gold, frankincense, and myrrh. Matthew 2:11

5

Mary said to the angel, "How will this happen since I am a virgin?" The angel said to Mary, "The Holy Spirit will come upon you, and the power of the Most High will cover you. For this reason the baby will be holy and will be called the Son of God." Luke 1:34-35

10

An angel of the Lord came to Joseph in a dream. The angel said, "Joseph, descendant of David, don't be afraid to take Mary as your wife, because the baby in her is from the Holy Spirit." Matthew 1:20

15

The Word became a human and lived among us. We saw his glory – the glory that belongs to the only Son of the Father – and he was full of grace and truth. John 1:14

20

The prophet wrote about this in the Scriptures: "But you, Bethlehem, in the land of Judah, are not just an insignificant village in Judah. A ruler will come from you who will be like a shepherd for my people Israel." Matthew 2:5-6

25

A child has been born to us; God has given a son to us. He will be responsible for leading the people. His name will be Wonderful Counselor, Powerful God, Father Who Lives Forever, Prince of Peace. Isaiah 9:6

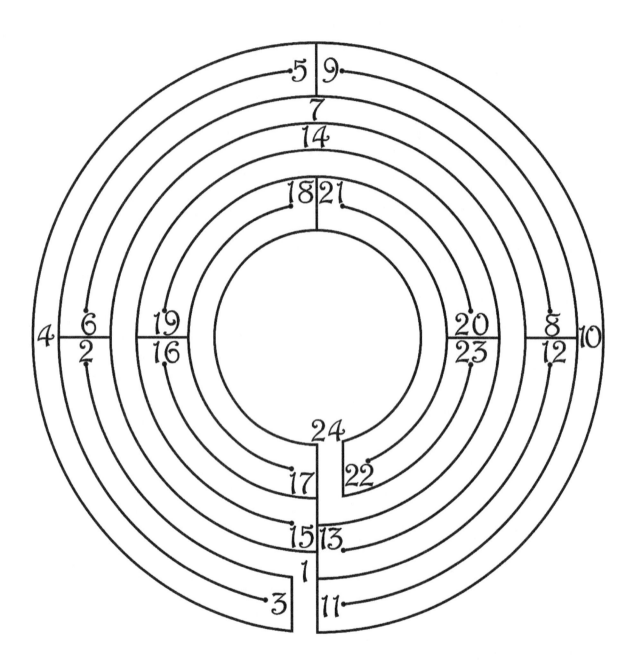

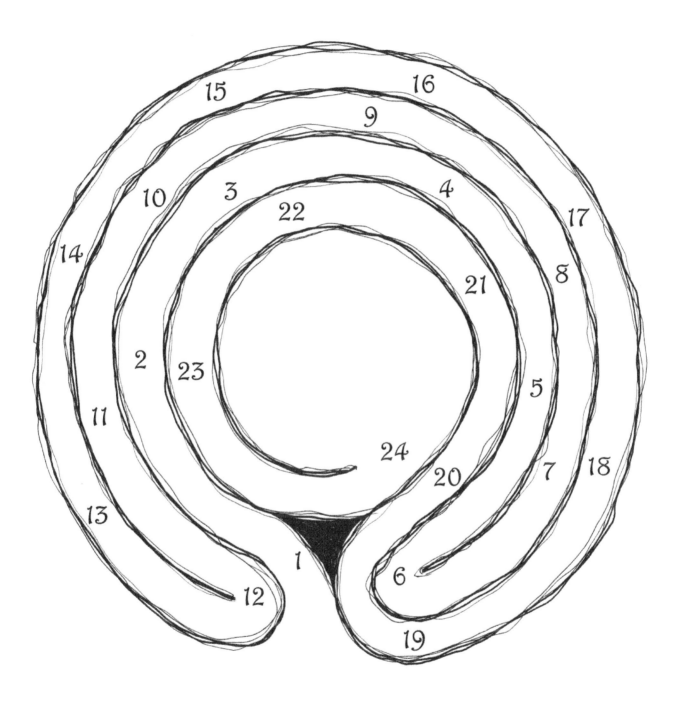

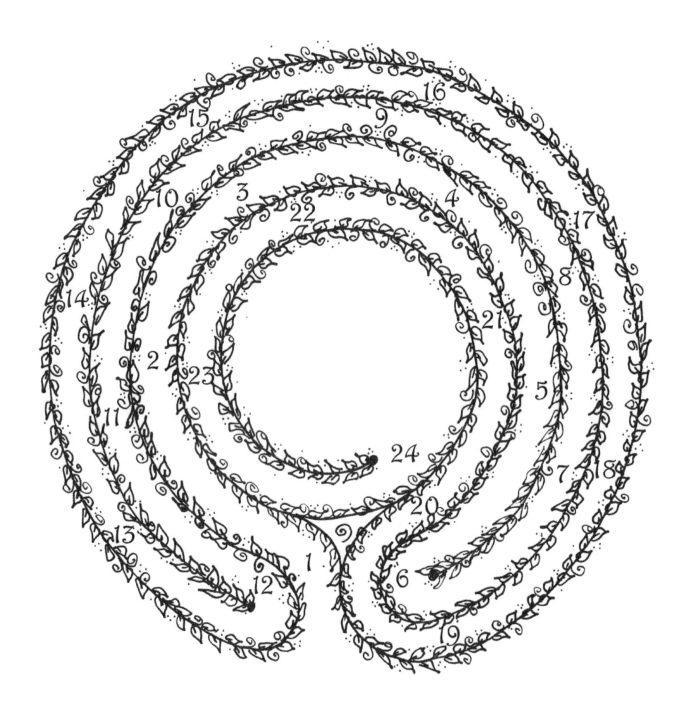

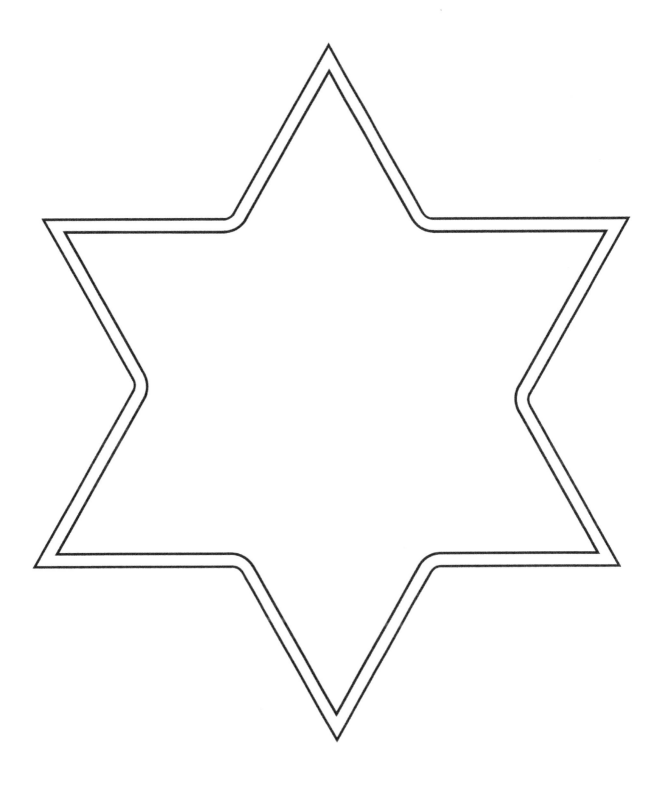

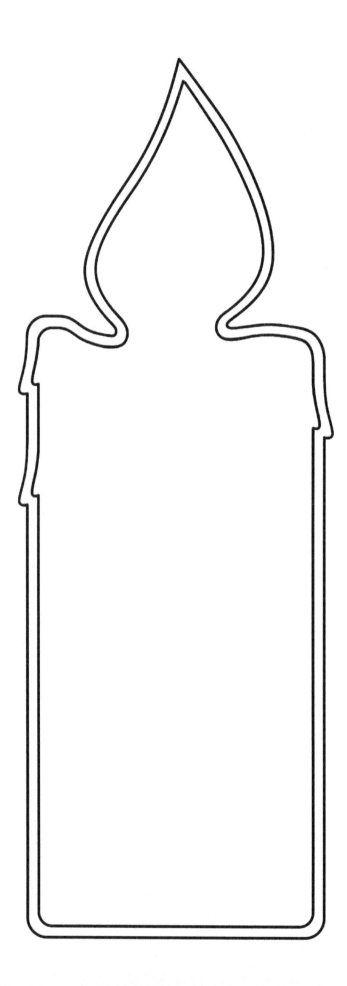

The Stuff at the Back

About the Author

Hi! I'm Fay.

Somehow I've ended up being a #1 bestselling Christian author – and no-one is more surprised than me!

My nice, sensible life got all shaken up a few years ago by Luke 9:59. A young man was making excuses for not following Jesus. "First let me bury my father", he said, with a sub-text of 'First let me inherit the family farm and get the business secure'. Reasonable, surely? Apparently not.

God is famed for his accuracy with a rolled-up newspaper, and this verse hit me with a deft Thwack! I had been saying the same thing. "First let me get my children into school. First let me get my career back up and running. First let me …" Oops. Time to get off my bum and, ummn, well, I'm still figuring that out. But a large part of it is to write.

The Reflectionary is my weekly blog of resources for interactive worship, based on readings from the Revised Common Lectionary. Everything is free, so pop along and help yourself at www.reflectionary.org. There, you can join our happy throng of subscribers and have posts sent straight to your inbox, or you can 'like' The Reflectionary on facebook.

The best of The Reflectionary makes it into book form, and one of those books shot straight to #1!

My two books of Bible sketches, *A Bucketful of Ideas for Church Drama*, and *A(nother) Bucketful of* … etc., are available in paperback and Kindle from your local Amazon store or via my author website. I write for other folks too, such as the URC's daily devotions and prayer handbook.

Besides all that, I'm a graduate theology student at Wesley House, Cambridge. My main research interest is children's spirituality, and I have recently published on that topic in the academic journal, *Practical Theology*.

When not writing, I teach maths for a living and spend most of the rest of the time being creative. I live with my children in an untidy house in the middle of England full of noise and glue sticks and mess, which I blame on the kids, but it's me really.

Contact

If you have any questions, comments or feedback, I'd really love to hear from you. No, really, I would. After all, you, dear reader, are the very reason I write. Without you it would be like the UK's Eurovision entry … pointless.

You can drop me a line (fay@fayrowland.co.uk) and let me know how your advent is going, and may you have a joyful and peaceful Christmas.

blessings,

Fay

Printed in Great Britain
by Amazon

48125866R00052